W9-ADI-316

Play
Guitar
Today!

A Complete
Guide to
the Basics

by Jeff Schroedl and Doug Downing

Recording Credits:
Todd Greene, Producer
Jake Johnson, Engineer
Doug Boduch, Guitar
Scott Schroedl, Drums
Tom McGirr, Bass
Warren Wiegratz, Keyboards
Andy Dress, Narration

ISBN 0-634-03052-3

HAL•LEONARD®
CORPORATION
7777 W. BLUEMOUND RD. P.O. BOX 13819 MILWAUKEE, WI 53213

Visit Hal Leonard Online at
www.halleonard.com

Contents

Introduction

Welcome to *Play Guitar Today!*—the series designed to prepare you for any style of guitar playing, from rock to blues to jazz to classical. Whatever your taste in music, *Play Guitar Today!* will give you the start you need.

About the CD

It's easy and fun to play guitar, and the accompanying CD will make your learning even more enjoyable, as we take you step by step through each lesson and play each song along with a full band. Much like with a real lesson, the best way to learn this material is to read and practice a while first on your own, then listen to the CD. With *Play Guitar Today!*, you can learn at your own pace. If there is ever something that you don't quite understand the first time through, go back on the CD and listen again. Every musical track has been given a track number, so if you want to practice a song again, you can find it right away.

The Basics

The Parts of the Guitar

The guitar has been a popular instrument for hundreds of years because it is both versatile and portable—not to mention it sounds great!

Although there are many different kinds of guitars, they all fall into one of two basic categories: *acoustic* or *electric*. These two types are shown below. Find the one that most resembles your own guitar, and get acquainted with its parts.

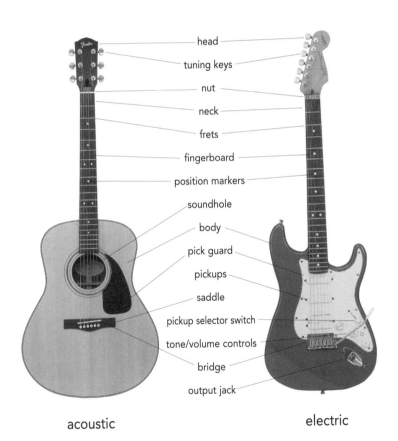

head
tuning keys
nut
neck
frets
fingerboard
position markers
soundhole
body
pick guard
pickups
saddle
pickup selector switch
tone/volume controls
bridge
output jack

acoustic   electric

How to Hold Your Guitar

Sitting is probably the mos
comfortable position when
first learning to play. Rest t
guitar on your right thigh a
hold it against the right sid
of your chest with your rigl
arm. If you want to raise th
neck to a more comfortabl
position, cross your legs—
find yourself a foot rest.

If your guitar has a strap, you may
prefer to stand. The basic position
of the guitar should remain the
same. Your hands must always be
free to move across the strings.
Therefore, don't hold the guitar
with your hands; support it with
your body or with a strap.

Your Right and Left Hands

When you play, you'll be striking the strings with a pick held in your right hand. To hold the pick properly, grip it between the thumb and index finger, keeping the rest of your hand relaxed and your fingers curved. The fingers not holding the pick may rest on the guitar for extra support.

Your left hand belongs on the neck of the guitar. It, too, should be relaxed. To help you get a feel for the correct hand placement, follow these suggestions:

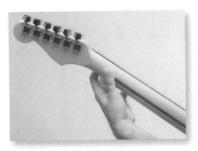

1. Place your thumb on the underside of the guitar neck.

2. Arch your fingers so that you will be able to reach all the strings more easily.

3. Avoid letting the palm of your hand touch the neck of the guitar.

Playing Is Easy

You produce sounds on your guitar either by **strumming** several string at once or by **picking** one string at a time. Take a minute to get a feel this. With the pick in your right hand, use a downward motion and ge strum the strings. Practice this several times to get the feel of the pick and the strings. Then try picking the strings one at a time from bottor to top.

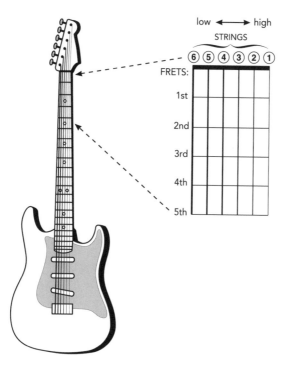

Notice that some strir sound higher and son sound lower? Each ha different **pitch**. Pitch i the highness or lowne of a sound. On the gu tar, the strings are nur bered 1 through 6, fro the highest-sounding string (the thinnest) to the lowest-sounding o (the thickest).

As you can see, the fre of the guitar are also numbered, from low (near the nut) to high (near the bridge). Fretting higher up the neck produces sounds a higher pitch, fretting lower on the neck pro- duces sounds of a lowe pitch.

The fingers of your left hand are also numbered, for convenience:

Tuning Up

If you loosen a string by turning its tuning key, the pitch will become lower; if you tighten the string, the pitch will become higher. When two pitches sound exactly the same, they are said to be *in tune*. There are many ways to get your guitar in tune: you may use an electronic tuner, a piano, a pitch pipe, a tuning fork—you can even tune your guitar purely to itself. For now, however, listen to the CD to help you tune your instrument. The guitar's six open strings should be tuned to these pitches:

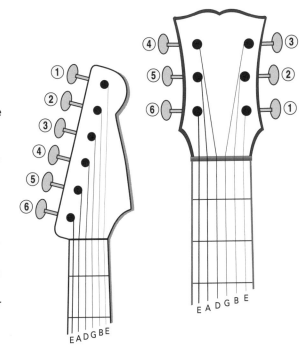

⑥ ⑤ ④ ③ ② ①
E–A–D–G–B–E
low ←——→ high

Here are a few tips to help get you started:

- Whether tightening or loosening a string, turn the peg slowly so that you can concentrate on the changes in pitch. You may need to pick the string repeatedly to compare it.

- As you're tuning a string, you may notice that a series of pulsating **beat waves** becomes audible. These beat waves can actually help you tune: they'll slow down as you get closer to bringing two pitches together, and they'll stop completely once the two pitches are exactly the same.

- Instead of tuning a string *down* to pitch, tune it *up*. Tuning up allows you to stretch the string into place, which will help it stay in tune longer. So, if you begin with a string that is too high in pitch, tune it down first, and then bring it back up to pitch.

How to Read Music

Musical sounds are indicated by symbols called **notes**. Notes come in shapes and sizes, but every note has two important components: pitch and rhythm.

Pitch

Pitch (the highness or lowness of a note) is indicated by the placement of the note on a **staff**, a set of five lines and four spaces. Notes higher on the staff are higher in pitch; notes lower on the staff are lower in pitch.

the staff

To name the notes on the staff, we use the first seven letters of the alphabet: *A–B–C–D–E–F–G*. Adding a **treble clef** assigns a particular note name to each line and space on the staff, centered around the p

treble clef

E F G A B C D E F

G, the second line of the staff.

E G B D F
Every Good Boy Does Fine

F A C E
"FACE"

An easy way to remember the pitches on the lines is "Every Good Boy Does Fine." For the spaces, spell "**FACE**."

Rhythm

Rhythm refers to how long, or for how many beats, a note lasts. This is indicated with the following symbols:

whole note
(four beats)

half note
(two beats)

quarter note
(one beat)

To help you keep track of the beats in a piece of music, the staff is divided into **measures** (or "bars"). A **time signature** (or "meter") at the beginning of the staff indicates how many beats you can expect to find in each measure.

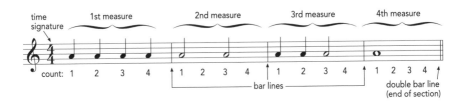

4/4 is perhaps the most common time signature. The top number ("4") tells you how many beats there are in each measure; the bottom number ("4") tells you what type of note value receives one beat. In 4/4 time, there are four beats in each measure, and each beat is worth one quarter note.

The First String: E

The first three notes we'll learn on the guitar are all found on the high E string.

E

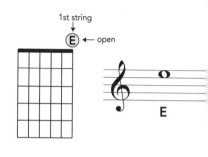

■ Your first note, E, is an "open-string" tone. There's nothing to fret—simply strike the open first string with your pick.

F

▶ Notice that your finger actually belongs *directly behind each fret*. If you place it on top of the fret, or too far back, you'll have difficulty getting a full, clear sound.

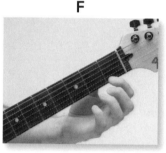

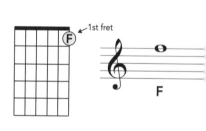

■ For the next note F, place your first finger on the first string directly behind the first fret, and strike the string with your pick.

G

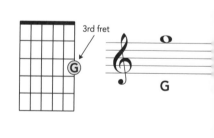

■ To play the note G, place your third finger on the first string directly behind the third fret, and strike the string with your pick.

Learn to recognize these notes both on the fretboard and on the staff. Then, when you're comfortable playing the notes individually, try this short exercise. Speak the note names aloud as you play (e.g., "E, F, G, F...").

E–F–G

ck 5

Of course, the best way to really learn these notes is to use them in some tunes. So let's do it. Start slowly with the following melodies, and concentrate on keeping your tempo nice and even. Practice these several times on your own before you try playing along with the audio.

First Song

ck 6

Keeping Time

Having trouble keeping a steady rhythm? Try tapping and counting along with each song. If the guitar is resting on your right leg, use your left foot to tap. Each time the foot comes down marks one beat. In 4/4 time, tap your foot four times in each measure, and count "1, 2, 3, 4." The first beat of each measure should be accented slightly—this is indicated below by the symbol ">."

count and tap: 1   2   3   4   1   2   3   4   1   2   3   4   1   2   3   4

Second Song

► If you like, read through each song *with-out* your guitar at first: Tap the beat with your foot, count out loud, and *clap* through the rhythms.

Third Song

Even though you don't actually use your left hand to fret the open strin E, keep that hand on the guitar in "ready position," with your thumb o the back of the neck. This will allow you to fret the other notes that mu more quickly.

Three-Note Rock

Try to keep your eyes on the page, instead of on your guitar.

Spiraling Downward

Downstrokes

Remember, you should be striking the strings with a downward motion of your pick. This is called a **downstroke**, sometimes indicated with the symbol ⊓.

As you play through these tunes, strive for efficiency and relaxation in your right-hand picking motion. It doesn't take much movement to get a good, solid downstroke.

| before stroke | after stroke |

The Second String: B

Track 11

Your next three notes are all played on the second string B. You might want to check your tuning on that string before going any further.

B

► Notice that we're using the same fret positions as on the E string: open, 1st, and 3rd.

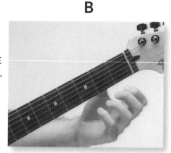

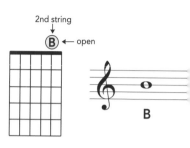

2nd string

(B) ← open

B

■ To play the note B, just strike the open second string.

C

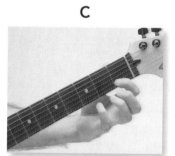

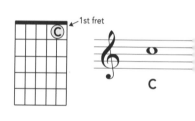

1st fret

(C)

C

■ To play the note C, place your first finger directly behind the first fret.

D

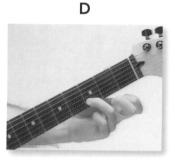

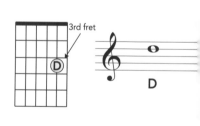

3rd fret

(D)

D

■ To play the note D, place your third finger at the third fret.

Practice these next exercises several times, slow and easy. Then play them along with the audio.

B-C-D

Three to Get Ready

TIP: Be sure to keep your left-hand fingers curved but relaxed, and use just your fingertips to fret the notes. Here's a test: you should be able to play any note on the B string without muffling the open E above it. If you can't do this, you're probably laying your fingers too flat across the fretboard.

Now here are some tunes to practice all six notes you've learned so far. Don't be afraid to review E, F, and G again before tackling these!

Two-String Rock

Fingering Tip

When moving from a lower note to a higher note on the same string, try leaving the lower note depressed. For example, on the first string, leave your first finger on F while you put your third finger on G. Now, to go back to F, you simply lift your third finger. This way, you don't have to find the first fret all over again—you're already there!

Track 15

Ode to Joy

Track 16

Jingle Bells

By the way, it's much better to practice just a little every day than it is to cram everything into one long session—your fingers and your mind need time to develop.

Black Dog Blues

Rests

In addition to notes, songs may also contain silences, or *rests*—beats in which you play nothing at all. A rest is a musical pause. Rests are like notes in that they have their own rhythmic values, instructing you how long (or for how many beats) to pause:

whole rest	half rest	quarter rest
(four beats)	(two beats)	(one beat)

Try tapping, counting, and playing this exercise.

ack 18

Rest Easy

19

Here's something else to consider: When you encounter a rest, you may need to stop any previous notes from sounding. To do this, try the following:

- For an open-string note, like E, touch the string lightly with your left-hand finger(s).

- For a fretted note, like F, decrease the pressure of your left-hand finger on the string.

Rock 'n' Rest

Track 19

The Pickup

Instead of starting a song with a rest, a *pickup* measure is sometimes used. In a pickup, any opening rests are simply deleted. So, if a pickup has only one beat, you count "1, 2, 3" and start playing on beat 4.

When the Saints Go Marching In

Track 20

► Often, when a song begins with a pickup measure, the missing beat(s) can be found in the song's final measure.

missing beat from
pickup measure

20

The Third String: G

ck 21

For this string, we'll learn just two notes, including one that's on the second fret. Don't forget to check your tuning.

G

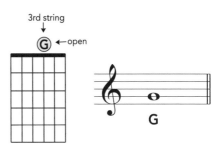

3rd string

G ←open

G

■ To play the note G, strike the open third string.

A

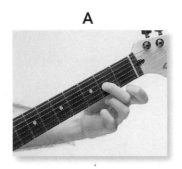

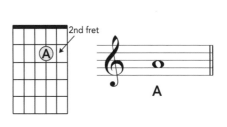

2nd fret

A

A

■ To play the note A, place your second finger at the second fret.

Notice that we're learning another G note—since the musical alphabet contains only the letters A through G, this type of repetition will eventually occur with all the note names.

Let's practice our two new notes, G and A.

ck 22

Two-Note Jam

Three-String Review

Here's all the notes we've learned so far, from G to G. That's eight notes in all!

G   A   B   C   D   E   F   G

Play through these, then play just the low G and the high G, and notice how similar they sound. Two different notes with the same letter name like this are called octaves. The prefix "oct" comes from the Latin word for "eight."

Remember to practice these next songs slowly at first. Ideally, you shoul be able to read and play the notes in time, without having to slow down or stop in the middle of a song. Speed up the tempo as you become more confident with the notes, and then play along with the band.

Track 23

Brother John

Track 24

► Notice the pickup measure on this song. You actually begin playing on beat 3.

Red River Rock

Aura Lee

ack 25

this: put
guitar
and just
the note
s of the
("G, C, B,
A, D...").

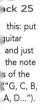

Michael, Row Your Boat Ashore

ck 26

Here Comes the Guitarist

ck 27

If your fingertips hurt, take a break. The more you practice, the faster they'll toughen up, but it takes time.

Two New Notes: F♯ and C♯

Notice that we skipped the second fret on both the first and second strings. Let's go back and grab those notes.

F♯

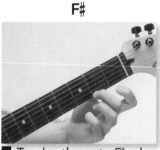

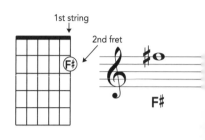

■ To play the note F♯, place your second finger on the first string, behind the second fret.

C♯

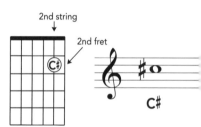

■ To play the note C♯, place your second finger on the second string, behind the second fret.

These are "sharped" notes. A **sharp** (♯) raises the pitch of a note by one fret. If you think about it, it makes sense: on the first string, one fret higher than F is F-sharp; on the second string, one fret higher than C is C-sharp.

Sharps, Flats, and Naturals

Sharps are part of a group of musical symbols called **accidentals**, which raise or lower the pitch of a note:

> A **sharp** (♯) raises the pitch of a note by one fret.
> A **flat** (♭) lowers the pitch of a note by one fret.

A **natural** (♮) cancels a previous sharp or flat.

In musical terms, the distance of one fret is called a **half step**. When a song requires a note to be a half step higher or lower, you'll see a sharp (♯), flat (♭), or natural (♮) sign in front of it. This tells you to raise or lower the note for *that measure only*.

Sharpen Up

k 29

this short
se with
ew notes.

Rockin' Sharps

k 30

Secret Agent Sharp

k 31

ce again,
keep your
on the
, not your
s.

The Fourth String: D

Track 32

The fourth string is like the third string in that we'll skip over the first fret—but this time we'll get three notes.

D

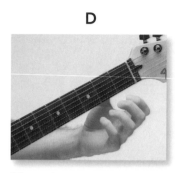

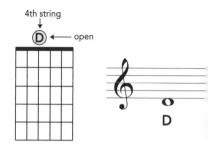

4th string

D ◄— open

D

■ To play the note D, strike the open fourth string.

E

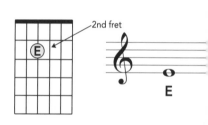

2nd fret

E

E

■ To play the note E, place your second finger at the second fret.

F

► Sound familiar? The new D, E, and F, sound *one octave lower* than the old D, E, and F.

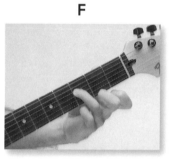

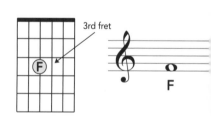

3rd fret

F

F

■ To play the note F, place your third finger at the third fret.

D-E-F

Now, try your new notes in some more songs. Practice them slowly at first.

D-String Riff

word *riff*
for a
d instru-
figure,
cal idea.

Easy Does It

Crosswalk Blues

u like,
D string
t on
ng.

Eighth Notes

If you divide a quarter note in half, what you get is an **eighth note**. An eighth note looks like a quarter note, but with a flag on it.

Two eighth notes equal one quarter note. To help you keep track of the beat, consecutive eighths are connected with a beam.

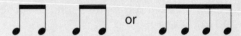

To count eighth notes, divide the beat into two, and use "and" between the beats. Practice this, first by counting out loud while tapping your foot on the beat, and then by playing the notes while counting and tapping.

Eighth rests are the same, but you pause instead of playing.

Now try some songs that use eighth notes. Keep that foot tapping!

Alouette

28

Eighth-Note Rock

38

3/4 Time

The next song is in **3/4** meter. That is, three beats (quarter notes) per measure.

three beats per measure
quarter note (1/4) gets one beat

count: 1   2   3   1   2   3   1   2   3   1   2   3

3/4 time feels very different from 4/4 time. Be sure to accent the first beat of each measure, just slightly; this will help you feel the new meter.

Amazing Grace

39

Two More Notes: F♯ and B♭

From the strings that we already know, let's add two more new notes: and B♭.

F♯

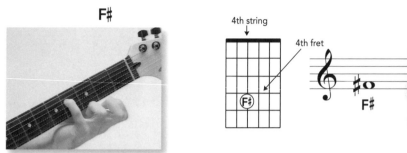

■ To play the note F♯, place your fourth finger on the fourth string, behind the fourth fret.

B♭

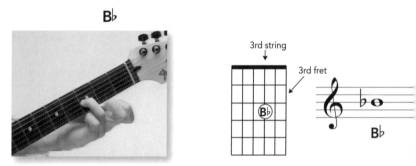

■ To play the note B♭ place your third finger on the third string, behind the third fret.

Londonderry Air

Snake Charmer

Minuet

epeat signs (|: :|) tell you to repeat everything in between them.
only one sign appears (:|), repeat from the beginning of the piece.

Rolling Rock

43

ember:
al sign
cels an
tal on a
turning
original

repeat back
to beginning

God Rest Ye Merry Gentlemen

Bourrée

Ties and Dots

The *tie* is a curved line that connects two notes of the same pitch. When you see a tie, play the first note and then hold it for the total value of both notes.

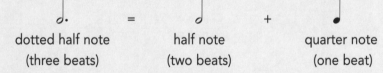

Ties are useful when you need to extend the value of a note across a bar line.

Another way to extend the value of a note is to use a **dot**. A dot extends any note by one-half its value. Most common is the dotted half note:

dotted half note	=	half note	+	quarter note
(three beats)		(two beats)		(one beat)

You'll encounter the dotted half note in many songs, especially those that use 3/4 meter.

It Came Upon a Midnight Clear

The Fifth String: A

Are you still in tune? Then it's time for another string. Your new notes B, and C, are all played on the fifth string. Notice that these notes all make use of **ledger lines**, which extend the staff downward, allowing to notate these lower pitches.

A

► Fingering-wise, the fifth string is just like the fourth: It uses open, 2nd, and 3rd fret positions.

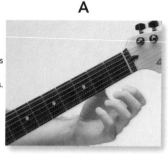

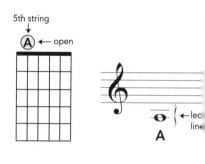

- To play the note A, strike the open fifth string.

B

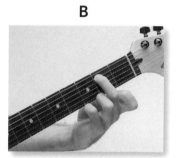

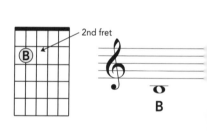

- To play the note B, place your second finger at the second fret.

C

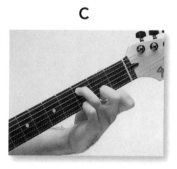

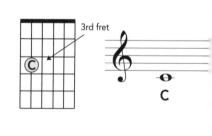

- To play the note C, place your third finger at the third fret.

Practice your new A, B, and C. Take it slow.

A-B-C

47

Cruisin'

48

Surfin'

49

Fallin' Down

50

Greensleeves

Track 51

Nine Hundred Miles

Track 52

► This next song is in 2/4 time. That is, two beats (quarter notes) per measure.

Alternate Picking

Alternate picking (a.k.a "the down/up stroke") is a good way of adding speed and facility to your guitar playing. It's actually a combination of two separate movements:

Downstroke Plucking or strumming the strings downward. This is how we've been playing all our tunes up to now. You should continue to use a downstroke for all notes that fall on a strong beat: "1," "2," "3," or "4." Remember the downstroke symbol is "⊓."

Upstroke Plucking or strumming the strings upward. An upstroke is generally used for an eighth note that falls on the second half of the beat—on the "and." The symbol for upstroke is "∨."

Try the following short exercises on the open high E string, using alternate picking.

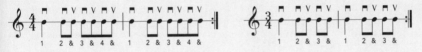

Now try this tune. First, play it with all downstrokes, then try the alternate picking method indicated.

Boogie Blues

k 53

The Sixth String: E

The notes E, F, and G are played on the sixth string of the guitar. As y●
practice these new notes, memorize their positions on the ledger line●

E

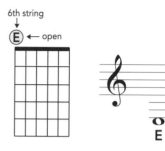

■ To play the note E, strike the open sixth string.

F

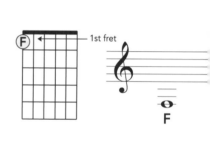

■ To play the note F, place your first finger at the first fret.

G

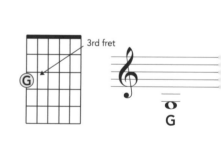

■ To play the note G, place your third finger at the third fret.

otice anything familiar here? These are the exact same notes and fingerings
ou learned for the first string, just two octaves lower:

he trick here will be reading and memorizing these notes on the staff. All
hose ledger lines can be tough. By the way, there's another set of E, F, and G
otes in between the first and sixth strings. Can you find it?

Take it nice and slow at first. Don't forget to let your eyes read ahead
of the notes you're actually playing; this can especially help on those
low strings.

Sixth-String Strut

k 54

alternate
g on
sive
notes.
ith down-
s for any
hat occurs
beat.

Bass Rock

k 55

Bye Bye, Johnny

Track 56

The Dotted Quarter Note

As we know, a dot lengthens a note by one half its time value. When a quarter note is followed by a dot, its time value is increased from 1 beat to 1 1/2 beats.

dotted quarter note (1 1/2 beats)   quarter note (1 beat)   eighth note (1/2 beat)

A dotted quarter note is usually followed by an eighth note. This pattern has a total time value of two beats.

To get more comfortable with counting dotted quarter notes, try the following rhythm exercise:

Rockin' Riff

Track 57

Hark! The Herald Angels Sing

2/2 Time

In **2/2** time, there are two beats per measure, and the half note gets the beat. This actually feels a lot like 4/4, but you only tap your foot twice in each measure.

Hail to the Guitarist

More Notes

Track 60

We may have learned all six strings, but let's double back and pick up just a few more notes before we move on. These first two are both flatted notes.

B♭

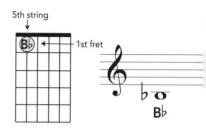

■ To play the note B♭, place your first finger on the fifth string, behind the first fret.

E♭

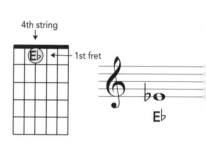

■ To play the note E♭, place your first finger on the fourth string behind the first fret.

Track 61

Minor Jam

Theme of Mystery

Silent Night

Now let's try a couple sharped notes.

G#

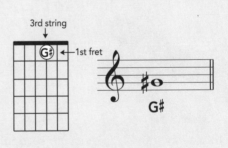

3rd string

G# ← 1st fret

G#

■ To play the note G#, place your first finger on the third string, behind the first fret.

C#

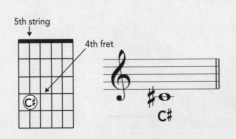

5th string

4th fret

C#

C#

■ To play the note C#, place your fourth finger on the fifth string, behind the fourth fret.

Nobody Knows the Troubles I've Seen

Track 64

John Brown's Body

Track 65

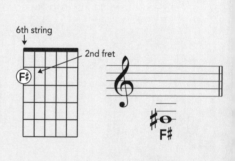

These last two notes are both on the sixth string.

F♯

■ To play the note F♯, place your second finger on the sixth string, behind the second fret.

G♯

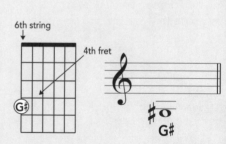

■ To play the note G♯, place your fourth finger on the sixth string, behind the fourth fret.

Blues in E

Low Groove

'atch the
s on this
Try to
ahead of
nusic.

Six-String Review

We've come a long way. In fact, we've learned just about *every* note in the guitar's open position. See if you can figure out the names of the two notes that we *haven't* covered.

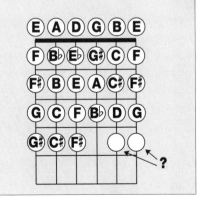

Major Chords

Track 68

Now that you've got a handle on all six strings, it's time to start learning about chords. *"What's a chord?"* you ask. A **chord** is three or more notes played simultaneously. We'll start off with three of the most common **major** chords. (More about what "major" means later…)

To play a chord, first get your left-hand fingers into position—the dots on each grid below tell you where to fret the strings, and the numbers tell you what fingers to use. Then, with your right hand, strum downward across the strings—but only those strings that are part of the chord.

C

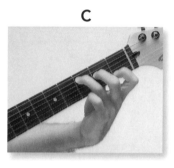

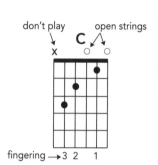

■ To play the C chord, get your fingers in place, then strum downward starting on the fifth string.

G

■ To play the G chord, get your fingers in place, then strum across all six strings.

D

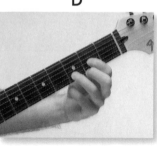

■ To play the D chord, get your fingers in place, and strum just the top four strings.

If a chord sounds bad, try playing through it again, but slowly, one string at a time. If you find a "problem string," readjust your finger or your hand position, and try again.

- **Are your fingers curved?** If you let them fall flat, they'll block other strings from sounding.
- **Is your thumb on the back of the guitar neck?** This will help you apply pressure to all the strings.
- **Are your fingers directly behind the frets?** This will give you a good, clear tone.

Tablature or "Tab"

We'll be learning a new type of musical notation to go with chords called *tablature*, or *"Tab"* for short. It consists of six lines, one for each string of your guitar. The numbers written on the lines indicate which fret to play in order to sound the correct notes.

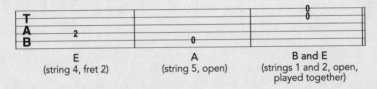

E	A	B and E
(string 4, fret 2)	(string 5, open)	(strings 1 and 2, open, played together)

Tab is a very popular notation method for contemporary guitar music and can be used for chords or melodies.

Tab This!

ack 69

Now try reading chords in notation and Tab.

Track 70

Let's Strum

Track 71

Let's Strum, Pt. 2

The next step is to try mixing the chords up. Chords arranged in sequence like this are called *progressions*. The number of possibilities are many. This chord progression moves from G to D to C to D and winds up back at G.

Track 72

Unplugged

► Don't be afraid to review these chords individually before playing this one!

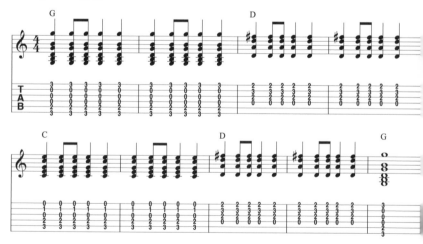

Here are a few very common progressions based on the same three chords: G, C, and D. You may recognize the first one, as it's similar to many rock songs, including "Louie, Louie" and "Wild Thing."

Wild Rock

k 73

Chord Moves

:k 74

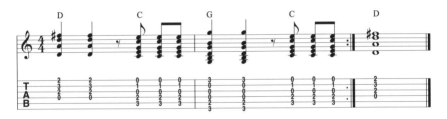

Chords can also be used to accompany a melody. Play the following songs by reading from the chord line. Strum once for each beat (that would be three strums per measure for the first two songs), and sing along with the melody.

Good Morning to All

:k 75

Beautiful Brown Eyes

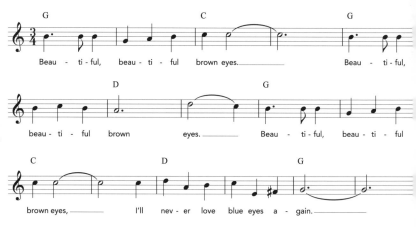

This next song is in 4/4 time, so strum four times per measure—or vary your strum pattern.

Buffalo Gals

Minor Chords

Since we just learned three major chords, let's even things out by learning three *minor* chords.

ck 78

Em

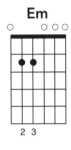

Em

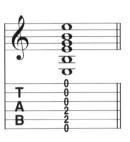

■ To play the Em chord, strum across all six strings.

Am

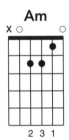

Am

■ To play the Am chord, begin your strum with the fifth string.

Dm

Dm

■ To play the Dm chord, strum just the top four strings.

Major vs. Minor

The difference between major and minor chords is in how they sound. Take a minute to compare two major and minor chords—like D and Dm. Notice how each one makes you feel? It's difficult to put into words, but generally we say that major chords have a strong, upbeat, or happy quality, while minor chords have a darker, sadder quality.

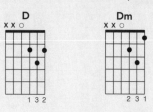

In terms of reading them, just remember that major chords use just the letter name (e.g., D), but minor chords use a letter name plus the suffix "m" (e.g., Dm).

Once again, when you feel comfortable with each chord individually, st experimenting with progressions.

Track 79

Let's Strum Again

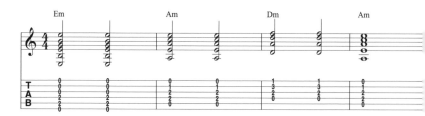

Track 80

Chord Trax #1

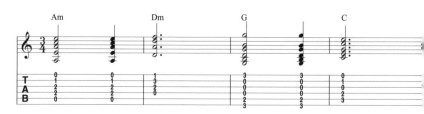

Chord Trax #2

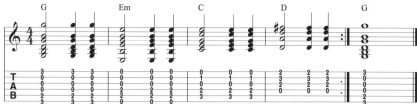

Chord Pairs

No matter how complex a progression, it always breaks down to movements from one chord to the next. As you move between different chords, if one or more fingers remain on the same note, allow them to stay pressed as you switch chords.

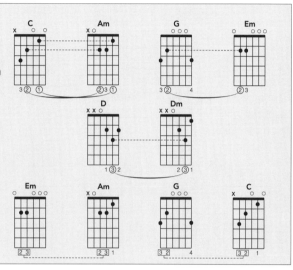

For the next example, try using an upstroke (V) for the last eighth note in each measure.

Chord Trax #3

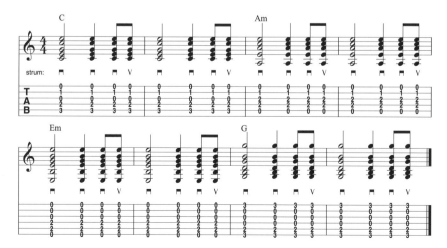

Strumming Partial Chords

When alternate strumming, don't worry about hitting every single note on the upstroke. Instead, just play two, three, or four notes of the chord—in other words, play whatever feels natural.

Chord Trax #4

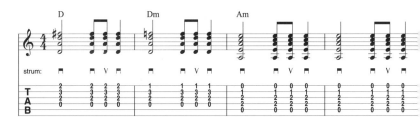

Chord Trax #5

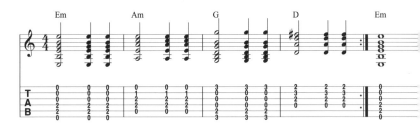

Once again, let's practice our new chords with some well-known melodies. Sing, and use the chord line to strum along.

When Johnny Comes Marching Home

Scarborough Fair

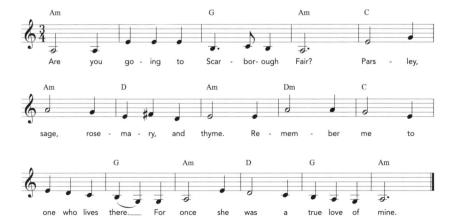

Slash Notation

Another way that you might see chord progressions written out is in *slash notation*. Slashes indicate how many beats each chord should be played; it's up to you to supply the strumming pattern. In the following progressions, first try strumming once for every slash (" / ") symbol. Then, follow the chord line and try variations of downstrokes and upstrokes.

Makin' Trax

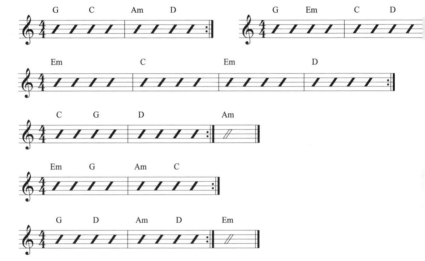

Practice chords daily (at least 15 minutes). Eventually, they'll become second nature. You'll instantly react when you see a chord symbol rather than trying to think of each fingering and note placement.

One More Note: A

Let's go back to that first string and grab one more note, the high A. This one will be played with the pinky.

A

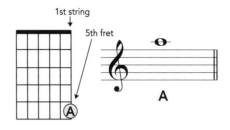

■ To play the high A, place your fourth finger on the first string, behind the fifth fret.

You'll probably want to move your hand up the fretboard, just a bit, to reach that fifth fret. Otherwise, you can opt to keep your hand in place, and stretch to reach the note. It's your choice.

Hittin' the High A

Track 88

From A to A to A

Now practice high A with the following scale:

A *scale* is an arrangement of notes in a specific, sequential pattern. Most scales use eight notes, with the top and the bottom notes being an octave apart. The one above spans two octaves.

And now a few more familiar tunes.

Track 89

Home Sweet Home

Auld Lang Syne

Track 90

House of the Rising Sun

Track 91

Power Chords

Finally, let's learn one more type of chord: the **power chord.** Each of these chords uses just two strings: one open and one fretted. Also, notice that power chords are labeled with the suffix "5."

E5

■ To play the E5 chord, think: sixth string, open, and fifth string, second fret.

A5

■ To play the A5 chord, think: fifth string, open, and fourth string, second fret.

D5

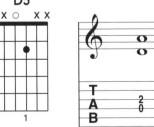

■ To play the D5 chord, think: fourth string, open, and third string, second fret.

Keep It Clean

Since these chords use just two strings at a time, they don't require a full strumming motion; just enough movement to pick the two strings. To keep any upper strings from accidentally sounding when playing these chords, try letting your left-hand fretting finger lay a little bit flat, so that it touches the string(s) above lightly.

Track 92

Warmin' Up

Track 93

Feelin' Good

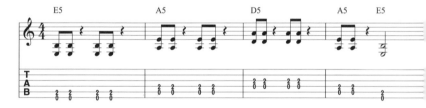

Track 94

Movin' and Shakin'

Review & More

Notes in First Position

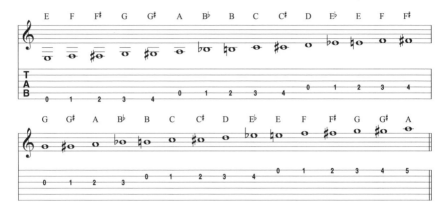

Chords

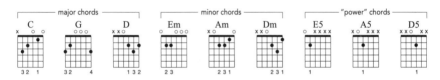

| major chords | | | minor chords | | | "power" chords | | |
| C | G | D | Em | Am | Dm | E5 | A5 | D5 |

How to Change a String

If you're missing a string, or your strings are old and dirty and need replacing, you'll need to know how to change a string. This diagram should help. Once you've inserted the string at the bridge, you need to wrap the other end around the tuning peg at the headstock.

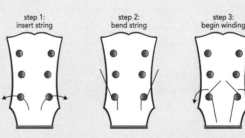

step 1: insert string
step 2: bend string
step 3: begin winding

To do this, first insert the string through the posthole. Then, bend it sharply to hold the string in place, and begin winding. You should allow enough slack at the start to wrap the string completely around the peg 3-4 times, and cut off any excess when you're finished.

Keep in mind, new strings need to be "stretched out" before you can expect them to hold their pitch. You can do this by pulling on each string one at a time with your fingers (over the pickups or soundhole, away from the body) after you've strung up your guitar, then retuning each of them to the correct pitch. Repeat this until each string stays in tune even after you've pulled on it.

Another Way to Tune Your Guitar

Here's another way to tune your guitar, or to check your tuning after you've tuned to the accompanying CD. This method proceeds from the 6th string to the 1st string, low to high:

1. Tune the 6th string E to a piano, a pitch pipe, an electronic tuner, the CD. If none of these is available, approximate E as best you c

2. Press the 6th string at the 5th fret. This is A. Tune the open 5th string to this pitch.

3. Press the 5th string at the 5th fret. This is D. Tune the open 4th string to this pitch.

4. Press the 4th string at the 5th fret. This is G. Tune the open 3rd string to this pitch.

5. Press the 3rd string at the 4th fret. This is B. Tune the open 2nd string to this pitch.

6. Press the 2nd string at the 5th fret. This is E. Tune the open 1st string to this pitch.

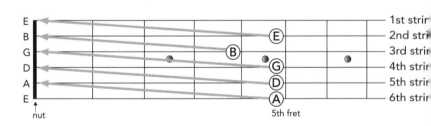

Bonus Songs

The last section of this book features five well-known pop and rock favorites. Before we begin, lets learn a few new things.

Song Structure

Most songs have different sections, that might be recognizable by any or all of the following:

- Introduction (or "Intro"): This is a short section at the beginning that "introduces" the song to the listeners.

- Verses: One of the main sections of the song—the part that includes most of the storyline—is the verse. There will usually be several verses, all with the same music but each with different lyrics.

- Chorus: Perhaps the most memorable section of the song is the chorus. Again, there might be several choruses, but each chorus will often have the same lyrics and music.

- Bridge: This section makes a transition from one part of a song to the next. For example, you may find a bridge between the chorus and next verse.

- Solos: Sometimes solos are played over the verse or chorus structure, but in some songs the solo section has its own structure. This is your time to shine!

- Outro: Similar to the "intro," this section brings the song to an end.

Endings

A few of the songs have some new symbols that you must understand before playing. Each of these symbols represents a different type of ending.

First and Second Endings

Play the song through to the first ending, repeat back to the first repeat sign, or beginning of the song (whichever is the case). Play through the song again, but skip the first ending and play the second ending.

D.S. al Coda

When you see these words, go back and repeat from this symbol: %

Play until you see the words "To Coda," then skip to the Coda, indicated by this symbol: ⊕

Now just finish the song.

Let It Be

Words and Music by John Lennon and Paul McCartney

Track 95

Additional Lyrics

And when the broken hearted people
living in the world agree,
there will be an answer, let it be.
For tho' they may be parted
there is still a chance that they will see,
there will be an answer, let it be.

3. And when the night is cloudy
    There is still a light that shines on me,
    Shine until tomorrow, let it be.
    I wake up to the sound of music
    Mother Mary comes to me,
    Speaking words of wisdom, let it be.

Brown Eyed Girl
Words and Music by Van Morrison

Additional Lyrics

Whatever happened to Tuesday and so slow,

Going down the old mine with a
  transistor radio?

Standing in the sunlight laughing,

Hiding behind a rainbow's wall,

Slipping and a-sliding

All along the waterfall

With you, my brown eyed girl.

You, my brown eyed girl.

Do you remember when we used to sing;

3. So hard to find my way, now that I'm all on
     my own.

   I saw you just the other day, my, how you
     have grown.

   Cast my memory back there, Lord,

   Sometimes I'm overcome thinking 'bout it.

   Making love in the green grass

   Behind the stadium

   With you, my brown eyed girl.

   You, my brown eyed girl.

   Do you remember when we used to sing;

Every Breath You Take

Written and Composed by Sting

Track 97

Additional Lyrics

2. Ev'ry single day, ev'ry word you say,
   Ev'ry game you play, ev'ry night you stay,
   I'll be watching you.

Time Is on My Side

Words and Music by Jerry Ragovoy

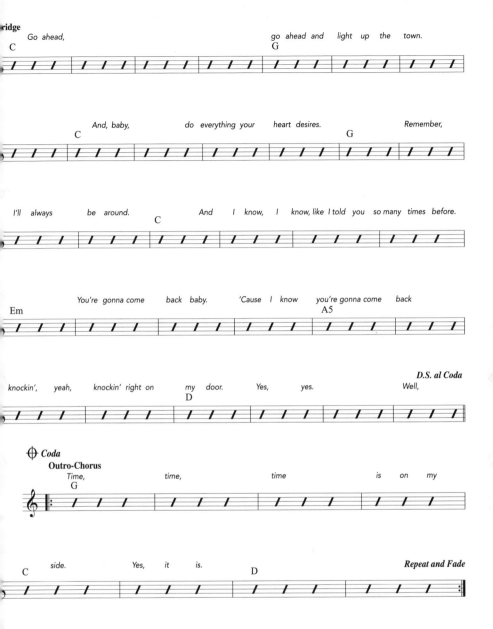

Go ahead, go ahead and light up the town.

C   G

And, baby, do everything your heart desires. Remember,

C   G

I'll always be around. And I know, I know, like I told you so many times before.

C

You're gonna come back baby. 'Cause I know you're gonna come back

Em   A5

knockin', yeah, knockin' right on my door. Yes, yes. Well,

D   *D.S. al Coda*

⊕ *Coda*
Outro-Chorus
Time, time, time is on my

G

side. Yes, it is. *Repeat and Fade*

C   D

Additional Lyrics

You're searchin' for good times, but just wait
and see.

You'll come runnin' back; I won't have to
worry no more.

You'll come runnin' back; spend the rest of my
life with you, babe.

You'll come runnin' back to me.

3. 'Cause I got the real love, the kind that
you need.

You'll come runnin' back; you said you
would, baby.

You'll come runnin' back; like I always said
you would.

You'll come runnin' back to me.

71

Wild Thing
Words and Music by Chip Taylor

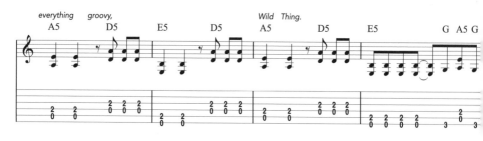

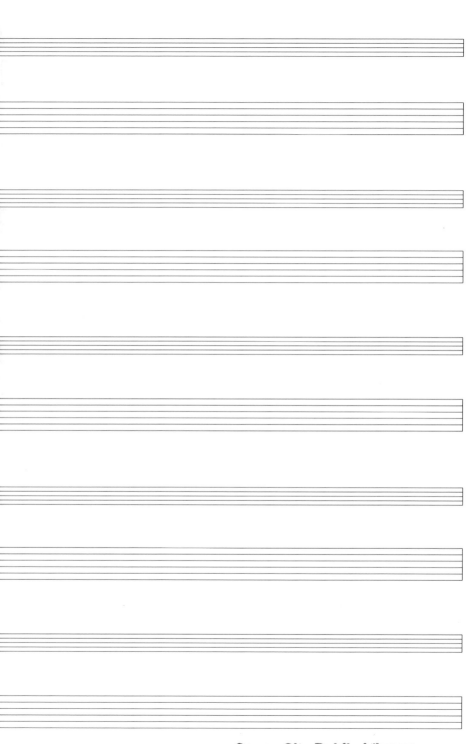

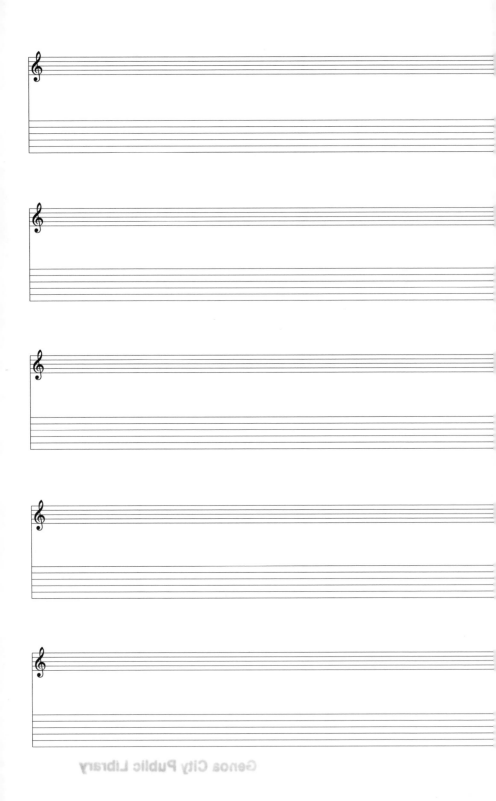